THE SCOTTISH QUOTATION BOOK

The
Scottish
Quotation
Book

A Literary Companion

Edited by
JOYCE AND MAURICE LINDSAY

ROBERT HALE · LONDON

Preface and selection © *Joyce and Maurice Lindsay 1991*
First published in Great Britain 1991

ISBN 0 7090 4679 0

Robert Hale Limited
Clerkenwell House
Clerkenwell Green
London EC1R 0HT

Photoset in Goudy by
Derek Doyle & Associates, Mold, Clwyd.
Printed and bound in Hong Kong
by Bookbuilders Ltd.

Preface

I like to have quotations ready for every occasion – they give one's ideas so pat, and save one the trouble of finding expression adequate to one's feelings.

ROBERT BURNS
Letter to Clarinda, 14 January 1788

We have tried to present as broad a picture as possible of Scotland as it has been seen down the ages by travellers, hostile and friendly, and by the Scots themselves, as well as to reflect something of the native wit and wisdom. Inevitably, in a country that produced the religious Reformation in the sixteenth century, and both the economist Adam Smith and the philosopher David Hume in the eighteenth, the serious side of the Scots temperament is widely reflected.

It would easily have been possible for us to fill such an anthology as this without searching much beyond the collected works of Robert Burns, Sir Walter Scott, Lord Byron (whose claim to Scottishness we do include) and Robert Louis Stevenson. We have resisted any such temptation, ranging through the writings of the lesser known as extensively as possible.

For the benefit of our non-Scottish readers we have glossed difficult Scots words. Where we have quoted from Middle Scots *writers, some of whose is endings have to be sounded for the sake of the rhythm (as, of course, they would have been originally), we have used the symbol īs.*

Since neither of us have Gaelic, and since Gaelic culture, though important, now represents only a small part of Scottish life, no Gaelic quotations are included here.

Scotland has made its distinctive contribution to European thought down the ages. Though sunken for a while during the nineteenth-century in inward-looking 'kailyairdism' (or 'cabbage-patching'), that mood has long since gone. That we do not quote more extensively from late-twentieth-century writers does not indicate any lack of our awareness of their considerable strengths, but is partly the consequence of copyright difficulties, and partly, in the case of many contemporary poets, that their work does not readily lend itself to the dissection of pithy quotation.

Many of our friends have made useful suggestions, for which we were grateful, particularly Fran Walker, Charles McKean and George Bruce. Fran Walker and Joe Fisher (before he retired from command of the Glasgow Room in the Mitchell Library) were particularly helpful in suggesting illustrations.

We hope that our pleasure in putting The Scottish Quotation Book together may be shared by many readers.

We would like to express our gratitude to the authors and other holders of copyright material who freelygave us permission to include quotations from it in these pages. We have used every endeavour to trace all such copyright holders, and apologise if any have been inadvertently overlooked.

JOYCE AND MAURICE LINDSAY

For so long as one hundred men remain alive, we shall never under any conditions submit to the domination of the English. It is not for glory or riches or honours that we fight, but only for liberty, which no good man will consent to lose but with his life.

THE DECLARATION OF ARBROATH, 1320

Broderick Castle, Arran, in the eighteenth century seat
of the Dukes of Hamilton

This is my country,
The land that begat me,
These windy spaces
Are surely my own.
and those who here toil
In the sweat of their faces
Are flesh of my flesh
And bone of my bone.
     SIR ALEXANDER GRAY
     'Scotland.

The rose of all the world is not for me.
I want for my part
Only the little white rose of Scotland
That smells sharp and sweet, and breaks the heart.
     HUGH MACDIARMID
     'The Little White Rose'

What do you mean when you speak of Scotland?
The grey defeats that are dead and gone
behind the legends each generation
savours afresh but can't live on? ...

Scotland's a sense of change, an endless
becoming for which there was never a kind
of wholeness or ultimate category.
Scotland's an attitude of mind.
     MAURICE LINDSAY
     'Speaking of Scotland', *Collected Poems 1940–90*

This queer compromise between fairyland and battleground
which is the Border.
     H.V. MORTON
     In Search of Scotland, 1929

A mist of memory broods and floats,
The Border waters flow;
The air is full of ballad notes
Borne out of long ago.
ANDREW LANG
'Three Crests Against the Saffron Sky'

Drums in the Walligate, pipes in the air,
Come and hear the cryin' o' the Fair.

A' as it used to be, when I was a loon
On Common-ridin' day in the Muckle Toon.
HUGH MACDIARMID
A Drunk Man Looks at the Thistle, 1926

If thou wouldst view fair Melrose aright,
Go visit it by the pale moonlight;
For the gay beams of light some day
Gild, but to flout, the ruins grey.
SIR WALTER SCOTT
The Lay of the Last Minstrel, 1805

Living in Edinburgh there abides, above all things, a sense
of its beauty. Hill, crag, castle, rock, blue stretch of sea, the
picturesque ridge of the Old Town, the squares and terraces
of the New ... The quick life of today sounding among the
relics of antiquity, and over-shadowed by the august
traditions of a Kingdom, makes residence in Edinburgh
more impressive than in any other British city.
ALEXANDER SMITH
A Summer in Skye, 1865

That knuckle-end of England.

SYDNEY SMITH

Quoted in Lady Holland, *Memoir of Sydney Smith*, 1855

Edinburgh, even were its population as great as that of London, could never be merely a city. Here there must always be present the idea of the comparative littleness of all human works. Here, the proudest of palaces must be content to catch the shadows of mountains; and the grandest of fortresses to appear like the dwellings of pigmies, perched on the very bulwarks of creation.

JOHN GIBSON LOCKHART

Peter's Letters to his Kinsfolk, 1819

As this Town is situated on the borders of the sea, and surrounded by hills of an immense height, the currents of air are carried down between them with a rapidity and a violence that nothing can resist. It has frequently been known, that in the New Town of Edinburgh three or four people have been scarce able to shut the door of the house.

EDWARD TOPHAM

Letters from Edinburgh Written in the Years 1774 and 1775

In the evening twilight we went today to the palace [Holyrood House] where Queen Mary lived and loved ... The chapel close to it is now roofless; grass and ivy grow there; and at the broken altar Mary was crowned Queen of Scotland. Everything around is broken and mouldering, and the bright sky shines in. I believe I found today in that old chapel the beginning of my Scotch Symphony.

FELIX MENDELSSOHN-BARTHOLDY

letter to his parents, August 1829

Medieval Glasgow. Fiddlers Close, demolished during
slum clearance in 1878.

The Old Town, it is pretended, is the chief characteristic,
and, from a picturesque point of view, the liver-wing of
Edinburgh. It is one of the most common forms of
depreciation to throw cold water on the whole by adroit
over-commendation of a part, since everything worth
judging, whether it be a man, a work of art, or only a fine
city, must be judged upon its merits as a whole.

ROBERT LOUIS STEVENSON
Edinburgh: Picturesque Notes, 1889

I wish you were in Edinboro' with me – it is quite lovely – bits of it.

OSCAR WILDE
letter to E.W. Godwin, 17 December 1884

… Miss Brodie was an Edinburgh spinster of the deepest dye.

MURIEL SPARK
The Prime of Miss Jean Brodie, 1961

The inhabitants of Edinburgh are forever calling their beautiful city the modern Athens or the Northern Oxford or the Scottish Wigan or something that it isn't or, at least, has no business to be.

JAMES BRIDIE
One Way of Living, 1939

Be it granted to me to behold you again in dying,
Hills of home! and to hear again the call;
Hear about the graves of the martyrs the peewees crying,
And hear no more at all.

ROBERT LOUIS STEVENSON
'To S.R. Crockett'

There is a view of the town of Perth, coming from the South, where the Romans halted to admire, and cried out in one voice – *Ecce Tiberem*! I think they paid a very bad compliment to the Tay, as there can be no comparison between it.

THE HON. SARAH MURRAY
A Companion and Useful Guide to the Beauties of Scotland, 1799

Prince Charlie's farewell to Flora Macdonald,
his rescuer, on leaving Scotland

Edina! Scotia's darling seat!
ROBERT BURNS
'Address to Edinburgh'

This is the East coast with winter
Written into its constitution,
And so is very productive of men
Who do not wait for good
In case there is none.
GEORGE BRUCE
'Praising Aberdeenshire Farmers'

Old tales, old customs and old men's dreams
Observe this town. Memories abound.
In the mild misted air, and in the sharp air
Toga and gown walk the pier.
The past sleeps in the stones.
GEORGE BRUCE
'A Gateway to the Sea: St Andrews'

St Andrews by the Northern Sea,
A haunted town it is to me!
A little city, worn and grey,
The grey North Oceans girds it round,
And o'er the rocks and up the bay,
The long sea-rollers surge and sound.
    ANDREW LANG
    'Almae Matres'

Dundee, certainly now, and for many years past, the most blackguard place in Scotland ... a sink of atrocity, which no moral flushing seems capable of cleansing.
    LORD COCKBURN
    Circuit Journeys, 1888

The town is ill-built and is dirty beside
For with water it's scantily, badly supplied
By wells, where the servants, in filling their pails
Stand for hours, spreading scandal, and falsehoods and tales
And abounds so in smells that a stranger supposes
The people are very deficient in noses.
Their buildings, as though they'd been scanty of ground
Are crammed into corners that cannot be found.
    THOMAS HOOD
    'Dundee', *Verse Letters to his Aunts*, 1815

Truly, the most striking fact about the Dundonians is that there are so many of them.
    SINCLAIR GAUDIE
    Dundee: An Illustrated Architectural Guide, 1984

Ye may speak o' heavenly mansions, ye may say it wadna
grieve ye
When ye quit a world sae bonnie – but I canna jist be
sure,
For I'll hae to wait, I'm thinkin', or I see if I believe ye,
For my first braid blink o' Heaven an' my last o'
Kirriemuir.

    VIOLET JACOB
    'Kirrie'

Aberdeen and twal mile round,
Fife, and aa the lands about it,
Taen fae Scotland's runklet map,
Little's left, and wha's tae doubt it?
    TRADITIONAL RHYME

A day oot o' Aiberdeen is a day oot o' life.
    TRADITIONAL SAYING

The sea-gray toun, the stane-gray sea,
The cushat's croudle mells wi the sea-man's skirl
Whaur baith gae skaichan fish-guts doon the quays
Or scrannan crumbs in cracks o the thrang causeys,
A lichthous plays the lamp-post owre a close,
The traffic clappers through a fisher's clachan
Whaur aa the vennels spulyie names frae the sea,
And kirks and crans clamjamfrie,
Heaven and haven mixter-maxtered heave
To the sweel o the same saut tide.
    ALEXANDER SCOTT
    'Aberdeen, Heart of Stone'

I wish I were where Gadie rins
Many fragrant heath and yellow whins,
Or, brawlin' doun the bochy linns,
At the back o' Benachie.
JOHN PARK
'Where Gadie Rins'

Lord Aberdeen was quite touched when I told him I was so attached to the dear, dear Highlands and missed the fine hills so much. There is a great peculiarity about the Highlands and Highlanders; and they are such a chivalrous, fine, active people.
QUEEN VICTORIA
quoted in *Victoria in the Highlands* (ed. D. Duff, 1968)

After Royalty came Deeside was ruined. The rich came and built huge palaces to try to outshine Easter Balmoral ... In our fisher dress a group of us stood by the roadside near Crathie. The queen [Victoria] came by, she looked so sour you could have hung a jug on her mouth.
CHRISTIAN WATT
The Christian Watt Papers, 1926

O for the crags that are wild and majestic,
The steep, frowning glories of dark Lochnagar!
LORD BYRON
Hours of Idleness, 1807

The ruins of the cathedral of Elgin afforded us another proof of the waste of reformation. There is enough remaining to show, that it was once magnificent.
DR SAMUEL JOHNSON
A Journey to the Western Islands of Scotland, 1775

I go North to cold, to home, to Kinnaird,
Fit monument for our time.
This is the outermost edge of Buchan.
Inland the sea birds range,
The tree's leaf has salt upon it,
The tree turns to the low stone wall.
    GEORGE BRUCE
    'Kinnaird Head'

Light is the dominating factor in its scenery, and the town-dweller, on his arrival in Orkney, will screw up his eyes and ask where all the light is coming from. Except Hoy, there are no hills high enough to intercept it. There are no trees to diminish it. There is, on the entire circumference, the sea to reflect it.
    ERIC LINKLATER
    'Orkney', *Scottish Country* (ed. George Scott
    Moncrieff, 1935)

The farms have been mechanized; land which formerly it was impossible to cultivate has been brought under the plough all over Orkney. A first glance will show how fertile the soils are – a chequer-work of pasture and cultivation from the shore half-way up the hills. The fishermen have bigger boats; they can fish in moderately deep water. They have their own co-operative and so get a secure price for their cod and lobster and scallops. The life and prosperity of fishermen has always been more uncertain than the farmers'; probably it must be that way.
GEORGE MACKAY BROWN
    An Orkney Tapestry, 1969

The spirit of the Shetlands is not easily or speedily apprehended; one must accustom oneself patiently to a different aspect of the world, a different rhythm of life, before one fully understands how its variations from what we have been used to are counter-balanced by its own essential qualities. The lack of ostentatious appearances, the seeming bareness and reserve, make the Shetlands insusceptible of being readily or quickly understood; one must steep oneself in them, let them grow upon one, to savour them properly.

> HUGH MACDIARMID
> *The Uncanny Scot*, 1968

The Atlantic surge
Pours in among the stormy Hebridies.

> JAMES THOMSON
> 'Autumn', *The Seasons*, 1730

From the lone sheiling of the misty island
Mountains divide us, and the waste of seas –
Yet still the blood is strong, the heart is Highland,
And we in dreams behold the Hebridies.

> ANON
> *Blackwood's Magazine*, September 1829

Skye is often raining, but also fine:
hardly embodied; semi-transparent;
like living in a jelly fish lit up
with green light.

> VIRGINIA WOOLF
> postcard to Duncan Grant, 27 June 1938

IONA.

The old abbey of Iona, reroofed and restored this century

In Iona of my heart, Iona of my love, instead of monks'
voices shall be the lowing of cattle, but ere the world come
to an end, Iona shall be as it was.

ST COLUMBA
attributed prophecy, before 597

That man is little to be envied, whose patriotism would not
gain force upon the plain of *Marathon*, or whose piety
would not grow warmer among the ruins of Iona.

DR SAMUEL JOHNSON
from James Boswell's *Journal of a Tour to the Hebridies*,
1785

If I had my home on Iona, and lived there upon melancholy
as other people do on their rents, my darkest moment
would be when in that wide space that deals in nothing but
cliffs and seagulls, suddenly a curl of steam would appear,
followed by a ship, and finally by a gay party in veils and

frock-coats, who would look for an hour at the ruins and graves ... and then move off again. This highly unjustifiable joke ... would be as if the inhabitants of these old graves haunted the place in ludicrous disguise.

    FELIX MENDELSSOHN-BARTHOLDY

While I was at Inverness there was not a trace of its ancient castle, some person having lately removed the small remains of its ruins to build offices, or some other such thing, for his own convenience: What an Hottentot!

    THE HON. MRS SARAH MURRAY
    A Companian and Useful Guide to the Beauties of Scotland, 1799

I am very glad to have seen the Caledonian Canal, but don't want to see it again.

    MATTHEW ARNOLD
    letter to his wife, 11 September 1882

My heart's in the Highlands, my heart is not here,
My heart's in the Highlands, a-chasing the deer;
A-chasing the wild deer and following the roe,
My heart's in the Highlands wherever I go.

    ROBERT BURNS
    'My heart's in the Highlands', *Scots Musical Museum*, 1790

Castles draw in their horns. The stones are streaming
with fine Highland rain. A woman's struggling
against the sour wet wind in a black skirt.
Mist on the mountains. Waterfalls are pouring
their tons of water with a hollow roaring.
The phantom chieftains pass the heavy port ...
> IAIN CRICHTON SMITH
> 'Highland Portrait', *Thistles and Roses*, 1951

We are now in Oban, which is, as far as I have seen it, the
Ramsgate of the Highlands ... On every lamp post is a
notice, 'Please do not spit on the pavement'.
> VIRGINIA WOOLF
> letter to Vanessa Bell, 28 June 1938
> Out of doors, Oban is not a bad representation of
> Vanity Fair. Every variety of pleasure-seeker is to be
> found there and every variety of costume.
> ALEXANDER SMITH
> *A Summer in Skye*, 1865

The world was as it was
a million years ago.
The slaty stone
slept in its tinged and aboriginal iron.
The sky might flower a little, and the grass
perpetuate its sheep. But from the sea
the bare bleak islands rose, beyond the few
uneasy witticisms we let pursue
their desolate silences.
> IAIN CRICHTON SMITH
> *'At the Firth of Lorne'*

We drove to St Fillans, through the gloomy valley of Glencoe, as dark and dreadful as if the massacre had just taken place.

> BERTRAND RUSSELL
> *Autobiography*, 1967-9

Mile after mile the only sound that indicates life is the faint cry of a bird of prey from some storm-beaten pinnacle of rock. The progress of civilization, which had turned so many wastes into fields yellow with harvests or gay with apple-blossom, has only made Glencoe more desolate.

> LORD MACAULAY
> *History of England*, 1848-61

Many places have evil reputations. Few, at first seeming, live up to those reputations ... In Scotland, the Pass of Glencoe, the scene of the infamous massacre, is one of them.

> ALISTAIR MACLEAN
> *When Eight Bells Toll*, 1966

That old lonely lovely way of living
in Highland places – twenty years a-growing,
twenty years flowering, twenty years declining –
father to son, mother to daughter giving
ripe tradition; peaceful bounty flowing;
one harmony, all tones of life combing –
old, wise ways, passed like the dust blowing.

> DOUGLAS YOUNG
> 'For the Old Highlands', *Auntran Blads*, 1943

In the highlands, in the country places,
Where the old plain men have rosy faces,
And the young fair maidens
Quiet eyes.
  ROBERT LOUIS STEVENSON
  Songs of Travel, 1896

What exactly *are* the Trossachs? They are a pass, a gorge, a
hollow way that stretches out beside a little river between
two masses of rock, those of Ben A'an and Ben Venue,
which stand like watchmen next to Loch Katrine with their
broad backs to Loch Achray ...
  THEODOR FONTANE
  Beyond the Tweed, Pictures and Letters from Scotland,
  1860

The mountains are extatic, and ought to be visited in
pilgrimage once a year. None but those monstrous creatures
of God know how to join so much beauty with so much
horror.
  THOMAS GRAY
  letter to William Mason, 2 November 1765

Ben Lomond ... in its simple majesty, cloud-capt or bare,
and descending to a point at the head of the lake, shews the
Trossacs beyond, tumbling about their blue ridges like
woods waving; to the left is the Cobbler, whose top is like a
Castle shattered in pieces and nodding to its ruins and at

your side rise the shapes of round pastoral hills, green, fleeced with herds, and retiring into mountainous bays and upland valleys, where solitude and peace might make their lasting home, if peace were to be found in solitude!

> WILLIAM HAZLITT
> Letter to James Sheridan Knowles, 1822

Stirling, like a huge brooch, clasps Highlands and Lowlands together.

> ALEXANDER SMITH
> *A Summer in Skye*, 1865

Loch Lomond lies quite near to Glasgow. Nice Glaswegians motor out there and admire the scenery and calculate its horse-power and drink whisky and chaff one another in genteelly Anglicised Glaswegianisms.

> LEWIS GRASSIC GIBBON
> *Scottish Scene (with Hugh MacDiarmid)*, 1934

Had Loch Lomond been in a happier climate, it would have been the boast of wealth and vanity to own one of the little spots which it encloses, and to have employed upon it all the arts of embellishment. But, as it is, the islets which court the gazer at a distance disgust him at his approach when he finds, instead of soft lawns and shady thickets nothing more than uncultivated ruggedness.

> DR SAMUEL JOHNSON, 1775
> *A Journey to the Western Isles of Scotland*, 1775

In point of picturesque beauty, Loch Lomond is probably surpassed by few lakes in Europe.

> CHRISTOPHER NORTH
> *The Land of Burns*, 1841

The superb Loch Lomond, the fine sunlight that gilded its waters, the silvery rocks that skirted its shores, the flowery and verdant mosses, the black oxen, the white sheep, the shepherds beneath the pines ... I shall often dream of Tarbet, even in the midst of lovely Italy with its oranges, its myrtles, its laurels, and its jessamines.

B. FAUJAS ST FOND
Travels in England and Scotland, 1784

A voyage down the Clyde is enough to make anybody happy; nowhere can the home tourist, at all events, behold, in the course of one day, such a succession and variety of beautiful, romantic and majestic scenery.

JOHN GIBSON LOCKHART
Memoirs of the Life of Sir Walter Scott, 1837-8

Under the darkness nothing seems to stir;
The lilac bush like a conspirator
Shams dead upon the lawn, and there
Above the flagstaff the Great Bear
Hangs as a portent over Helensburgh.

W.H. AUDEN
'The Watchers', February 1932

Pure stream, in whose transparent wave
My youthful limbs I want to lave.
No torrents stain thy limpid source,
No rocks impale thy dimpling course
That warbles sweetly o'er its bed,
With white, round, polished pebbles spread ...

TOBIAS SMOLLETT
'Ode to Leven Water', 1771

25

Dumbarton Castle, that Gibraltar of antiquity.
> JOHN GALT
> *The Ayrshire Legatees*, 1821

The suburbs of Glasgow extend very far, houses on each side of the highway – all ugly, and the inhabitants of the city dirty. The roads are very wide; and everything seems to tell of the neighbourhood of a large town.
> DOROTHY WORDSWORTH
> Journal, 1803

Glasgow to Thee thy neighbouring towns give place,
'Bove them thou lifts thine head with comely grace.
Scarce in the spacious earth can any see
A city that's more beautiful than thee.
> DR ARTHUR JOHNSTON
> translated from the Latin by I.B., 1605

Glasgow is to outward appearance, the prettiest and most uniform town that I ever saw; and I believe there is nothing like it in Britain.
> EDMUND BURT
> *Letters from a Gentleman*, 1715

O Glasgow! famed for ilka thing
That heart can wish or siller bring!
> JOHN MAYNE
> 'Glasgow', *Two Scots Poems*, 1783

The old college of Glasgow, destroyed with the medieval city, *c.* 1870

City! I am true son of thine;
Ne'er dwelt I where great mornings shine
Around the bleating pens;
Ne'er by the rivulets I strayed
and ne'er upon my childhood weighed
The silence of the glens.
Instead of shores where ocean beats
I hear the ebb and glow of streets.
    ALEXANDER SMITH
    'Glasgow', *A Life Drama and Other Poems*, 1857

The misty smoke and the tenements of Glasgow, caught in
the light, made a magic of their own.
    GUY McCRONE
    The Philistines, 1947

Clammy midnight, moonless mist,
A cigarette glows and fades on a cough,
Meth-men mutter on benches,
pawed by river fog, Monteith Row
sweats coldly, crumbles, dies
slowly. All shadows are aliens.
    EDWIN MORGAN
    'Glasgow Green'

I belong to Glasgow –
Dear old Glasgow town!
But what's the matter wi' Glasgow?
For it's going round and round.
I'm only a common old working chap,
As anyone can see,
But when I get a couple of drinks on a Saturday,
Glasgow belongs to me!
    WILL FYFFE, 1921

Glasgow ... the vomit of a cataleptic commercialism.
    JAMES LESLIE MITCHELL
    The Thirteenth Disciple, 1931

Where the broad marsh, a shuddering surface lies,
Fair Greenock's spires in new-born beauty rise.
    JOHN WILSON
    The Clyde, 1764

This grey town
That pipes the morning up before the lark
With shrieking steam, and from a hundred stalks
Lacquers the sooty sky; where hammers clang
On iron hulls, and cranes in harbour creak,
Rattle and swing whole cargoes on their necks …
> JOHN DAVIDSON
> of Greenock, 'Ballad of the Making of a Poet'

Auld Ayr, whom ne'er a town surpasses,
For honest men and bonny lasses.
> ROBERT BURNS
> *Tam o' Shanter*, 1791

For of what avail can the ceremonies of a royal funeral be
… at Irvine, where Kings never die?
> JOHN GALT
> *The Ayrshire Legatees*, 1821

… the Mull of Cantire, the Scottish equivalent of the Bay
of Biscay …
> JAMES BRIDIE
> *One Way of Living*, 1939

Without Kintyre Scotland wouldn't have a leg to stand on.
> TRADITIONAL KINTYRE SAYING

Macduff: Stands Scotland where it did?
Rosse: Alas, poore Country,
Almost afraid to know itselfe. It cannot
Be call'd our mother but our grave; where nothing'
But who knows nothing, is once seen to smile.
> WILLIAM SHAKESPEARE
> *Macbeth*, 1605-6

Treacherous Scotland, to no interest true.
>   JOHN DRYDEN
>   'Death of Oliver Cromwell', 1658

The lande of Scotland hath plenty of vytail and corn but
not abundant as is the realm of England, for this land is in
many places steryll. The people be tall men and hardy, but
unfaythfull of promise.
>   ROGER BARLOW
>   *A Brief Summe of Geographie, c.* 1540

O Caledonia! stern and wild,
Meet nurse for a poetic child!
Land of brown heath and shaggy wood,
Land of the mountain and the flood ...
>   SIR WALTER SCOTT
>   *The Lay of the Last Minstrel*, 1805

Scotland! thy weather's like a modish wife!
Thy winds and rains forever are at strife:
So, termagant, a while, her thunder tries,
And, when she can no longer scold – she cries.
>   AARON HILL
>   *Writ on a Window, in the Highlands of Scotland, c.* 1728

A Scottish mist may wet an Englishman to the skin, – that
is, small mischiefs in the beginning, if not seasonably
prevented, may prove very dangerous.
>   THOMAS FULLER
>   *History of the Worthies of England*, 1662

Man alone seems to be the only creature who has arrived to the natural size in this poor soil; every part of the country presents the same dismal landscape, no grove nor brook lends music to cheer the stranger, or to make the inhabitants forget their poverty; yet with all these disadvantages to call him down to humility a Scotchman is one of the proudest things alive.

OLIVER GOLDSMITH
letter to Robert Bryant, Edinburgh, 26 September 1753

A French writer mentions, as a proof of Shakespeare's attention to particulars, his allusion to climate in Scotland in the words, 'Hail, hail, all hail! – Grète, grète, toute grète.'

THOMAS MOORE
journal, 16 April 1821

Scotland's cauld and grey, you say,
But it's no' ill to prove
Oor dourest hills are only
Rainbows at a'e remove.

HUGH MACDIARMID
'To Circumjack Cencrastus', 1930

The Scots are steadfast – not their clime.

THOMAS CAMPBELL
'The Pilgrim of Glencoe', 1842

31

Scotsmen are metaphysical and emotional, they are sceptical and mystical, they are romantic and ironic, they are cruel and tender, and full of mirth and despair.
RACHAEL ANNAND TAYLOR
William Dunbar, 1931

Scotchmen seem to think it's a credit to them to be Scotch.
W. SOMERSET MAUGHAM
A Writer's Notebook, 1900

The Scots have a slight tincture of letters, with which they make a parade among people who are more illiterate than themselves; but they may be said to float on the surface of science, and they have made very small advances in the useful arts.
TOBIAS SMOLLETT
Lieutenant Lismahagow in *Humphry Clinker*, 1771

The Scotch are a nation of gentlemen.
GEORGE IV

Scotland is renowned as the home of the most ambitious race in the world.
FREDERIC EDWIN SMITH, EARL OF BIRKENHEAD
Rectorial address, Aberdeen University, 1928

'Guid gi'e us a guid conceit o' oursel's', is the Scotsman's most earnest prayer.
JAMES BRIDIE
One Way of Living, 1939

A Scottish man is ay wise behind the hand.
JOHN RAY
A Compleat Collection of English Proverbs, 1670

Much (said he) may be made of a Scotchman, if he is caught young.

SAMUEL JOHNSON
from James Boswell's *The Life of Samuel Johnson*, 1791

The Lowland Scot differs from the rest of mankind in that he has no Unconscious Mind. He is aware and critical of all levels of his consciousness, even when he is asleep or tipsy. He is an expert upon himself, as a result of wary and continuous observation, into three planes – the Intellectual Plane, the Moral Plane and the Physical Plane ... He has considerable evidence that the consciousness of his neighbour is not so tidily marshalled. His neighbours are orra bodies; queer folk; all out of step but our Jock; amusing; even partly explicable; but disordered and *abnormal*.

JAMES BRIDIE
One Way of Living, 1939

Scotland seemed at a glance ancient, grimy, lush, mysterious and mannerly ... Lost causes abounded.

JOHN UPDIKE
Bech is Back, 1983

The common people in Scotland, who are fed with oatmeal, are in general neither so strong, nor so handsome as the same rank of people in England, who are fed with wheaten bread. They neither work so well, nor look so well; and as there is not the same difference between the people of fashion in the two countries, experience would seem to show, that the food of the common people of Scotland is not so suitable to the human constitution as that of their neighbours of the same rank in England.

ADAM SMITH
The Wealth of Nations, 1776

A drunken husband helped home by a wrathful wife

I think it possible that all Scots are illegitimate, Scotsmen being so mean and Scotswomen so generous.
EDWIN MUIR
Scottish Journey, 1935

No nation has so large a stock of benevolence as the Scotch. Their temper stands anything but an attack on their climate. They would even have you believe they can ripen fruit; and, to be candid, I must own in remarkably warm summers, I have tasted peaches that made excellent pickles.
SYDNEY SMITH
Lady Holland, *Memoir of Sydney Smith*, 1855

The natural love of your native country suld be inseperably rooted in your hearts, considerand that your lives, your bodies, your habitation, your friends, your livings and sustenance, your hail, your peace, your refuge, the rest of your eild [age] and your sepulture is in it.

> ANON
> *The Complaynt of Scotland*, 1549

None can destroy Scotland save Scotland itself ... My Lord, patricide is a greater crime than parricide.

> LORD BELHAVEN
> opposing the Union of 1707

The enemies of Scottish Nationalism are not the English, for they were ever a great and generous folk, quick to respond when justice calls. Our real enemies are among us, born without imagination.

> R.B. CUNNINGHAME GRAHAM
> speech at Bannockburn, 21 June 1930

I wondered not when I was told
The venal Scot his country sold:
I rather very much admire
How he could ever find a buyer.

> ANON
> from Nichol's *Select Collection of Poems*, 1780

While the warm blood bedews my veins
And unimpared remembrance reigns,
Resentment at my country's fate
Within my filial breast shall beat;
And, spite of her insulting foe,
My sympathising verse shall flow:
'Mourn, hapless Caledonia, mourn,
Thy banish'd peace, thy laurels torn'.
>   TOBIAS SMOLLETT
>   'The Tears of Scotland'
>   written after Culloden, 1746

Caledonia's ours.
And well I know within that bastard land
Hath wisdom's goddess never held command;
A barren soil, where Nature's germs, confined
To stern sterility can stint the mind;
Whose thistle well betrays the niggard earth.
Emblem of all to whom the land gives birth;
Each genial influence nurtured to resist;
A land of meanness, sophistry and mist.
>   LORD BYRON
>   *The Curse of Minerva*, 1811

Courage beyond the point and obdurate pride
Made us a nation, robbed us of a nation.
Defiance, absolute and myriad-eyed,
That could not pluck the palm plucked our damnation.
>   EDWIN MUIR
>   'Scotland, 1941', *The Narrow Place*, 1941

In all things pertaining to this land that move the Scot to his marrow, you will observe this note of tragedy, this singing of lost causes, of dead years, of death.

NEIL M. GUNN
Whisky and Scotland, 1935

For that is the mark of the Scot of all classes: that he stands in an attitude towards the past unthinkable to Englishmen, and remembers and cherishes the memory of his forebears, good or bad; and there burns alive in him a sense of identity with the dead even to the twentieth generation.

ROBERT LOUIS STEVENSON
Weir of Hermiston, 1894

For I am half a Scot by birth, and bred
A whole one, and my heart flies to my head
As Auld Lang Syne brings Scotland, one and all,
Scotch plaids, Scotch snoods, the blue hills and clear streams,
The Dee, the Don, Balgownie's Brig's black wall,
All my boy feelings, all my gentler dreams
Of what I then dreamt, clothed in their own pall,
Like Banquo's offspring. Floating past me seems
My childhood in this childishness of mine:
I care not – 'tis a glimpse of Auld Lang Syne.

LORD BYRON
Don Juan, 1819-24

With Byron and with Lermontov
Romantic Scotland's in the grave.

G.S. FRASER
'Home Town Elegy', 1944

For God's sake, sir, let us remain as Nature made us, Englishmen, Irishmen and Scotchmen, with something like the impress of our several countries upon each!

SIR WALTER SCOTT
Letters of Malachi Malagrowther, 1826

Just as the conservation of natural resources, perhaps at the last moment, has become a matter of acute concern on a worldwide scale, so we in Scotland begin to know and value what we have been, what we are, and what we might have become.

GEORGE BRUCE
from *The Future of Scotland*, ed. R. Underwood, 1977

Boswell: I do indeed come from Scotland, but I cannot help it ...
Johnson: That, sir, I find, is what a great many of your countrymen cannot help.

JAMES BOSWELL
The Life of Samuel Johnson, 1791

I have been trying all my life to like Scotchmen, and am obliged to desist from the experiment in despair ... Between the affirmative and the negative there is no border-line ... He cannot compromise or understand middle actions. There is but a right and a wrong.

CHARLES LAMB
Essays of Elia, 1823-33

A Scotchman must be a very sturdy moralist, who does not love Scotland better than truth: he will always love it better than inquiry; and if falsehood flatters his vanity, will not be very diligent to detect it.

> DR SAMUEL JOHNSON
> *A Journey to the Western Isles of Scotland*, 1775

We have no damned fellow feeling at all, and look at ourselves with the eye of a Toulouse Lautrec appraising an obscene old toe-rag doing the double-split.

> HUGH MACDIARMID
> *The Uncanny Scot*, 1968

Sir, it is not so much to be lamented that Old England is lost, as that the Scots have found it.

> DR SAMUEL JOHNSON
> from James Boswell's *The Life of Samuel Johnson*, 1791

Seeing Scotland, Madam, is only seeing a worse England.

> DR SAMUEL JOHNSON
> letter, 7 April 1778

I would do anything for you, Scotland, save
– Even tho' your true line should be wi' such –
Become like ninety per cent o' Scots;
That 'ud be askin' faur owre much.

> HUGH MACDIARMID
> 'Towards a New Scotland IV'

Land of the omnipotent No.

> ALAN BOLD
> 'A Memory of Death'

But, Sir, let me tell you, the noblest prospect which a Scotchman ever sees, is the high road that leads to England.

DR SAMUEL JOHNSON
from James Boswell's *The Life of Samuel Johnson*, 1791

Scotland is the country above all others that I have seen, in which a man of imagination may carve out his own pleasures; there are so many *inhabited* solitudes.

DOROTHY WORDSWORTH
journal, August 1803

So this is your Scotland. It is rather nice, but dampish and Northern and one shrinks a trifle inside one's skin. For these countries one should be an amphibian.

D.H. LAWRENCE
Letter to the Hon. Dorothy Brett, 14 August 1928

Once you get the hang of it and apprehend the type, it is a most beautiful and admirable little country – fit, for 'distinction', etc., to make up a trio with Italy and Greece.

HENRY JAMES
letter to his sister Alice, 15 September 1878

It is never difficult to distinguish between a Scotsman with a grievance and a ray of sunshine.

P.G. WODEHOUSE
from Richard Usborne, *Wodehouse at Work*, 1961

When shall I see Scotland again? Never shall I forget the happy days I passed there amidst odious smells, barbarous sounds, bad suppers, excellent hearts and most enlightened and cultivated understanding.

SYDNEY SMITH
letter to Francis Jeffrey, 27 March 1814

God help England if she had no Scots to think for her!
GEORGE BERNARD SHAW
The Apple Cart, 1929

Let nae man think he can serve you, Scotland,
Withoot muckle trial and trouble to himsel'!
The slightest service to you compares
Wi' fetchin' a bit o' Heaven doon into Hell.
HUGH MACDIARMID
'Towards a New Scotland VIII', *Stony Limits and Other Verses*, 1934

Scotland has suffered in the past, and is suffering now, from too much England.
A.G. MACDONNELL
My Scotland, 1937

Scotland's worst disease is its appalling love for, and dependence on, the calculable.
HUGH MACDIARMID
'Scotia Irredenta'

Minds like ours, my dear James, must always be above national prejudices, and in all companies it gives me true pleasure to declare, that, as people, the English are very little indeed inferior to the Scots.

> CHRISTOPHER NORTH
> *Noctes Ambrosianae*, October 1826

Noo there's ane end of an auld sang.

> JAMES OGILVIE, 1st EARL OF SEAFIELD
> as he signed the Act of Union of 1707

By the union with England, the middling and inferior ranks of people in Scotland gained a compleat deliverance from the power of an aristocracy which had always oppressed them.

> ADAM SMITH
> *The Wealth of Nations*, 1776

> Fareweel to a' our Scottish fame,
> Fareweel our ancient glory
> Fareweel ev'n to the Scottish name,
> Sae famed in martial story!
> Now Sark rins over Solway's sands,
> An' Tweed rins to the ocean,
> To mark where England's province stands –
> Such a parcel of rogues in a nation!

> > ROBERT BURNS
> > 'Such a Parcel of Rogues in a Nation'

There is no art which one government sooner learns of another than of draining money from the pockets of the people.

> ADAM SMITH
> *The Wealth of Nations*, 1776

The family is the foundation of everything – the root out of which the social world grows. Break it up and you have as certainly introduced a corrupting poison into the framework of the community, as if you had inoculated the human frame with a deadly and malignant agent that destroys the very tissues of life.

> HUGH MILLER
> 'Our Working Classes'
> quoted in George Rosie, *Outrage and Order*, 1854

Then let us pray that come it may
(As come it will for a' that)
That sense and worth o'er a' the earth
Shall bear the gree for a' that!
For a' that, and a' that,
It's comin' yet for a' that,
That man to man the warld o'er
Shall brithers be for a' that.

> ROBERT BURNS
> 'A Man's a Man for a' that'

The English who have never crossed the Tweed, imagine erroneously, that Scotch ladies are not remarkable for personal attractions; but, I can declare with safe conscience, I never saw so many handsome females together.

> TOBIAS SMOLLETT
> *Humphry Clinker*, 1771

I have always been of the opinion, that none make better wives than the ladies of Scotland.

> JAMES THOMSON
> letter to his sister Jean, 4 October 1747

Love, though a very acute disorder in Andalusia, puts on a very chronic shape in these high northern latitudes; for first the lover must prove *metaphysically* that he ought to; and then in the fifth or sixth year of courtship, or rather argument, if the summer is tolerably warm, and oat meal plenty, the fair one yields.

> SYDNEY SMITH
> letter to Lady Holland

Woman is the blood-royal of life: let there be slight degrees of precedency among them, but let them all be sacred.

> ROBERT BURNS
> letter to Deborah Duff Davies, 6 April 1793

I hate a woman who seems to be hermetically sealed in the lower regions.

> SYDNEY SMITH
> of an Edinburgh lady, Mrs Aprece
> *Lady Holland, Memoir of Sydney Smith*, 1855

Behave yoursel' before folk,
Behave yoursel' before folk
And dinna be sae rude tae me
As kiss me sae before folk.
It wouldna gie me meikle pain,
Gin we were seen and heard by nane,
To tak a kiss or gie you ain,
But gudesakes! no before folk.

> ALEXANDER ROGER
> *Whistlebinkie*, 1846

Love is a very papithatick thing, as well as troublesome and tiresome.

> MARJORIE FLEMING ('PET MARJORIE')

I'm o'er young, I'm o'er young,
I'm o'er young to marry yet!
I'm o'er young, 'twod be a sin
To tak me frae my mammy yet.
ROBERT BURNS
'I'm o'er young'

Sleep I can get nane
For thinking on my dearie.
ROBERT BURNS
'Ay Waukin O'

Yestreen, when to the trembling string,
The dance gaed thro' the lighted ha',
To thee my fancy took its wing,
I sat, but neither heard nor saw;
Tho' this was fair, and that was braw,
And yon the toast of a' the town,
I sigh'd and said amang them a'
Ye are na Mary Morrison.
ROBERT BURNS
'Mary Morrison', *Scots Musical Museum*, 1788

O Jean, my Jean, when the bell ca's the congregation
Owre valley an' hill wi' the ding frae its iron mou',
When a'body's thochts is set on their ain salvation,
Mine's set on you.
VIOLET JACOB
'Tam i' the Kirk'

Forgot
Mysel.
ALEXANDER SCOTT
'Scotch Passion'
Scotched

Kissin' is the key o' love,
An' clappin' is the lock,
An' makin' o's the best thing
That e'er a young thing got.
SUNG TO THE BOY BURNS BY HIS MOTHER, AGNES
BROUN

Kiss'd yestreen, and kiss'd yestreen,
Up the Gallowgate, doun the Green:
I've woo'd wi' lords, and woo'd wi' lairds,
I've mooled wi' carls and moll'd wi' cairds,
I've kiss'd wi' priests – 'twas done i' the dark,
Twice in my gown and thrice in my sark;
But priest nor lord, nor loon can gie
Sic kindly kisses as he gae me.
ANON, EIGHTEENTH CENTURY

Glad am I, glad am I,
My mother is gone to Henislie.
Steek the dure and catch me,
Lay me doun and streche me,
Ye, gif I cry, hang me –
Ye, gif I die of the same,
Bury me bury me, in God's name.
ALEXANDER MONTGOMERIE
'Glad am I'

Blest, blest and happy be
Whose eyes behold her face,
But blessed more whose ears have heard
Thy speeches framed with grace;

And he is half a god
That these thy lips may kiss,
Yet god all whole that may enjoy
Thy body as it is.
    ANON, SIXTEENTH CENTURY

O lady, for thy constancy,
A faithful servant sall I be,
Thine honour to defend;
And I sall surely for thy sake,
As doth the turtle for her make,
Love to my lifīs end.
    ALEXANDER MONTGOMERIE
    'The Banks of Helicaon', *c.* 1597

The thing that may her please
My body sall fulfil;
Whatever her disease,
It does my body ill.
My bird, my bonny ane,
My tender babe venust
My luve, my life alane,
My liking and my lust,
    ALEXANDER SCOTT
    'My hairt is heich above'

A CELEBRATED JACOBITE BALLAD SINGER. CHARLIE LESLIE of ABERDEEN SHIRE. Who died 1782. Aged 105.

Mussel-mou'd Charlie, the last wandering Jacobite minstrel, died 1782

The kirk and state may join, an' tell
To do sic things I mauna;
The kirk an' state may gae to hell,
And I'll gae to my Anna.
ROBERT BURNS
'Yestreen I had a pint o' wine', c. 1790

Wae's me that e'er I made your bed!
Wae's me that e'er I saw ye!
For now I've lost my maidenhead,
And I ken na' how they ca' ye.

My name's weel kend in my ain countrie,
They ca' me the lintin' laddie;
And ye had na' been as willing as I,
Shame fa' them wad e'er hae bade ye.
ANON, EIGHTEENTH CENTURY

O wha my babie-clouts will buy?
Wha will tent me when I cry?
Wha will kiss me where I lie?
The rantin' dog, the daddie o't.
ROBERT BURNS
'O wha my babie-clouts will buy', *Scots Musical*
Museum, 1792

Cauld, cauld cools the lufe
That kindles owre het.
SIR JOHN FETHY
'Luve', c. 1548

In the blithe days of honeymoon,
With Kate's allurements smitten,
I lov'd her late, I lov'd her soon,
And call'd her dearest kitten.

But now my kitten's grown a cat,
And cross like other wives.
O! by my soul, my honest Katt,
I fear she has nine lives.
>   JAMES BOSWELL
>   'A Matrimonial Thought'

Luve is ane fervent fire,
Kendillt without desire:
Short plesour, lang displesour,
Repentance is the hire;
Ane puir tressour without messour:
Luve is ane fervent fire.
>   ALEXANDER SCOTT
>   'Lo, what it is to Luve', *Bannatyne Manuscript*, 1568

Yet have I been a lover by report,
Yea, I have died for love as others do,
But, prais'd be God, it was in such a sort
That I revived within an hour or two.
>   SIR ROBERT AYTON
>   'Upon Love', *c.* 1590

I think thair is na nation sa barbare whair it sall be refused
ony man to be heard to defend himself.
>   MAITLAND OF LETHINGTON
>   to the Duke of Norfolk

My hairt, sen thou may not her please,
Adieu, as good love comes as goes,
Go choose another and forget her;
God give him dolour and disease
That breks their hairt, and nocht the better.
ALEXANDER SCOTT
'To love unlovit', *Bannatyne Manuscript. c*, 1560

What can a young lassie, what shall a young lassie,
What can a young lassie dae wi' an auld man? ...
He's always compleenin' frae mornin to eenin',
He hoasts and he hirples the weary day lang;
He's doylt and he's dozin', his blude it is frozen,
O dreary's the night wi' a crazy auld man!
ROBERT BURNS

Their tricks an' craft hae put me daft,
They've taen me in an' a' that
But clear your decks, and here's – 'The Sex!'
I like the jads for a' that.
ROBERT BURNS
'Tho' women's minds like winter winds', 1790

Let them bring me prisoners, and I'll find them law.
ATTRIBUTED TO LORD BRAXFIELD
From Lord Cockburn, *Memorials of his Time*, 1856

Up the close and down the stair,
But and ben with Burke and Hare.
Burke's the butcher, Hare's the thief,
Knox the boy who buys the beef.
CONTEMPORARY JINGLE OF THE 1820s

Burke the murderer hanged this morning. The mob, which
was immense, demanded Knox and Hare but though greedy
for more victims, received with shouts the solitary wretch
who found his way to the gallows out of five or six who seem
not less guilty than he. But the story begins to stale,
although I believe a doggerel ballad upon it would be
popular, however brutal the wit.
SIR WALTER SCOTT
journal, 28 January 1829

I have heard a lawsuit compared to a country-dance, in
which, after a great bustle and regular confusion, the
parties stand still, all tired, just on the spot where thay
began.
JOHN GALT
The Ayreshire Legatees, 1821

A fig for those by law protected!
Liberty's a glorious feast!
Courts for cowards were erected,
Churches built to please the priest.
ROBERT BURNS
'The Jolly Beggars', 1799

Making ourselves masters of the English language is all very
proper, but we ought not to carry our compliance too far.
ANON
a contributor to *The Scots Magazine*, 1762

In ancient days, tradition says,
When knowledge much was stinted –
When few could teach and fewer preach,
And books were not yet printed –
What wise men thought, by prudence taught,
They pithily expounded;
And proverbs sage from age to age,
In every mouth abounded.
O blessings on the men of yore
Who wisdom thus augmented.
And left a store of useful lore
For human use invented.
> CHARLES, LORD NEAVES
> 'A Song of Proverbs, 1872

Give me a girl at an impressionable age, and she is mine for life.
> MURIEL SPARK
> *The Prime of Miss Jean Brodie*, 1961

There was no objection to the blue stocking, provided the petticoat came low enough.
> FRANCIS, LORD JEFFREY
> of Mrs Hamilton, author of *The Cottagers of Glenburnie*, 1808

There appears to be in the genius of the Scottish people – fostered no doubt by the abstract metaphysical education of their universities – a power of reducing human actions to formulae or principles.
> WALTER BAGEHOT
> *Literary Studies*, 1879

Luss, on Loch Lomond, a village in what was once Colquhon country

Man is a cooking animal; and in whatever situation he is found, it may be assumed as an axiom, that his progress in civilization has kept exact case with the degree of refinement he may have attained in the science of gastronomy.

SIR WALTER SCOTT
St Ronan's Well, 1823

She was one of that numerous class of ladies in Scotland who, virtuous and religious and every way estimable as they may be, do a great many things as if they believed the stomach to be by far the most important part in the construction of every human being.

> JOHN GIBSON LOCKHART
> *Adam Blair*, 1824

Some hae meat and canna eat
And some wad eat that want it.
But we hae meat and we can eat,
And sae the Lord be thankit.

> ATTRIBUTED TO ROBERT BURNS
> 'The Selkirk Grace'

The halesome parritch, chief o Scotia's food.

> ROBERT BURNS
> 'The Cotter's Saturday Night', 1785-6

Oats, n.s. A grain, which in England is generally given to horses, but in Scotland supports people.

> DR SAMUEL JOHNSON
> *A Dictionary of the English Language*, 1735

Oh ye cannae fling pieces oot a twenty storey flat,
Seven hundred hungry weans will testify to that.
If it's butter, cheese or jeely, if the breid is plain or pan,
The odds against it reaching earth are ninety-nine tae wan.

> ADAM McNAUGHTAN
> *The Scottish Folk Singer*

The ingle-neuk, wi' routh o' bannocks and bairns!
OLD SCOTTISH TOAST

A good breakfast as usual in Scotland, with Findon haddocks, eggs, sweetmeats and honey.
ROBERT SOUTHEY
Journal of a Tour in Scotland, 1819

My lords and lieges, let us all to dinner, for the cockie-leekie is a-cooling.
SIR WALTER SCOTT
The Fortunes of Nigel, 1822

During the early Celtic period, when adoration was paid to the waters, fish as food was taboo, and even after the introduction of Christianity, it continued for a time to be considered dangerous to the purity of the soul.
F. MARIAN McNEILL
The Scots Kitchen and Garden, 1929

Wha'll buy my caller herrin'?
They're bonnie fish and halesome farin';
Wha'll buy my caller herrin',
New drawn frae the Forth?
CAROLINE OLIPHANT, LADY NAIRNE
'Caller Herrin''

Though the casual Govan herring
Warns us by a sense unerring
That the dead need but interring –
Pisces Benedicte.

Taken fresh and all unspotted,
Rolled in vinegar and potted,
O, it tickles the parotid –
Pisces Benedicte.
WALTER ELLIOT
'Sestette to Fish'
Glasgow University Magazine, 1926

Meat in Scotland is frequently kept a fortnight smothered in oat meal and carefully wiped every day.
MRS DALGAIRNS
Practice in Cookery, 1829

I think, my friend, an fowk can get
A doll of roast beef pypin het,
And wi' red wine their wyson wet,
And cleathing clean,
And be nae sick, or drown'd in debt,
They're no too mean.
ALLAN RAMSAY
'Third Epistle to William Hamilton of Gilbertfield'

A Scot of poetic temperament, and without religious exhaltation, drops as if by nature into the public house. The picture may not be pleasing; but what else is a man to do in this dog's weather?
ROBERT LOUIS STEVENSON
Edinburgh, Picturesque Notes, 1889

I am not yet Scotchman enough to relish their singed sheep's head and haggis ... The first put me in mind of the history of Congo, in which I had read of negroes' heads sold publicly in the markets; the last, being a mess of minced lights, livers, suet, oatmeal, onions and pepper, enclosed in a sheep's stomach, had a very sudden effect upon mine ...

> TOBIAS SMOLLETT
> *Humphry Clinker*, 1771

Fair fa' your honest, sonsie face,
Great chieftain o' the puddin' race!
Aboon them a' ye tak your place,
Painch, tripe or thairm:
Weel are ye wordy o' a grace
As lang's my airm.

> ROBERT BURNS
> 'To a Haggis'

At the wedding of Shon Maclean
They blew with lungs of leather,
and blithesome was the strain
These pipers played together!
Moist with the mountain-dew,
Mighty of bone and thew,
Each with the bonnet blue,
Tartan, and blackcock feather;
And every piper was fou,
Twenty pipers together.

> ROBERT BUCHANAN
> 'The Wedding of Shon Maclean'

When the Lowlanders want to drink a cheer-upping cup, they go to the public house ... and call for a chopin of twopenny, which is a thin, yeasty beveridge, made of malt, not quite so strong as the table beer of England.

The Highlanders, on the contrary, despise this liquor and regale themselves with whisky, a malt spirit, as strong as geneva, which they swallow in great quantities, without any sign of inebriation ... I am told that it is given with great success to infants, as a cordial, in the confluent smallpox.

> TOBIAS SMOLLETT
> *Humphry Clinker*, 1771

Leeze me on drink, it gies us mair
Then either school or college:
It kindles wit, it waukens lear,
It pangs us fu' of knowledge,
Be't whisky gill or pennywheep
Or any stronger potion,
It never fails, in drinking deep,
To kittle up oor notion
By night or day.

> ROBERT BURNS
> 'The Holy Fair'

Gude claret best keeps out the cauld,
And drives away the winter soon;
It maks a man baith gash and bauld,
And haves his saul ayont the mune.

> ALLAN RAMSAY
> 'Look up to Pentland's tow'ring tap', Poems, 1721

Bold and erect the Caledonian stood,
Old was his mutton and his claret good;
Let him drink port, the English statesman cried –
He drank the poison and his spirit died.
JOHN GIBSON LOCKHART
Memoirs of the Life of Sir Walter Scott, 1837-8

Dr Johnson's absurdly crude view that claret is a wine for boys, with port allotted to men, was never shared in Scotland.
IVOR BROWN
I Give You My Word, 1945

The office of mingling the discordant elements of punch, into one sweet and harmonious whole, is perhaps the only one which calls into full play the sympathies and energies of a Glasgow gentleman. You read, in the solemnity of his countenance, his sense of deep responsibility which attaches to the duty he discharges ... how knowingly he squares the demons, and distinguishes between Jamaica rum, and Leeward Island, by the smell ... Then the snort and the snifter, and the smacking of the lips, with which the beveridge, when completed, is tasted by the whole party.
THOMAS HAMILTON
The Youth and Manhood of Cyril Thornton, 1827

O gude ale comes and gude ale goes,
Gude ale gars me sell my hose,
Sell my hose and pawn my shoon,
Gude ale hauds my her abune.
ANON, EIGHTEENTH CENTURY

Freedom and whisky gang thegither!
> ROBERT BURNS
> 'The Author's Earnest Cry and Prayer'

The proper drinking of Scotch whisky is more than indulgence; it is a toast to civilization, a tribute to the continuity of culture, a manifesto of man's determination to use the resources of nature to refresh mind and body and enjoy to the full the senses with which he has been endowed.
> DAVID DAICHES
> *Scotch Whisky*, 1969

These generous whiskies [the single malts], with their individual flavours, recall the world of hills and glens, of raging elements, of shelter and divine ease. The perfect moment of their reception is after bodily stress – or mental stress, if the body be sound. The essential oils that wind in the glass then uncurl their long fingers in lingering benediction and the whole works of creation are made manifest. At such a moment, the basest man would bless his enemy.
> NEIL M. GUNN
> *Whisky and Scotland*, 1935

Rabbie, wad'st thou were here – the warld hath need,
And Scotland mair sae, o the likes o thee!
The whisky that aince moved your lyre's become
A laxative for a' loquacity.
> HUGH MACDIARMID
> *A Drunk Man Looks at the Thistle*, 1926

There had been a carousing party at Castle Grant, many years ago, and as the evening advanced towards morning two Highlanders were in attendance to carry the guests upstairs ... One or two of the guests, however, whether from their abstinence or their superior strength of head, were walking upstairs and declined the proffered assistance. The attendants were astonished and indignantly exclaimed, 'Ach, it's sair changed times at Castle Grant, when gentlemans can gang to bed on their ain feet.'

> DEAN RAMSAY
> *Reminiscences of Scottish Life and Character*, 1858

At a prolonged drinking bout, one of the party remarked, 'What gars the Laird o' Garscadden luik sae gash?' 'Ou,' said his neighbour, the Laird of Kilmardinny, 'Garscadden's been wi' his Maker these twa hours; I saw him step awa', but I dinna like to disturb good company.'

> DEAN RAMSAY
> *Reminiscences of Scottish Life and Character*, 1858

Brissit brawnis and broken banes
Stryfe discorde and waistie wanis
Crukit in eild synhalt withal,
This are the bewties of the fute ball.
> MAITLAND FOLIO MANUSCRIPT, 1582

During nearly two hundred years from the Peace of Glasgow in 1502 to the Revolution of 1688, every reigning monarch of the Stuart line was a golfer.

> ROBERT BROWNING
> *History of Golf*, 1955

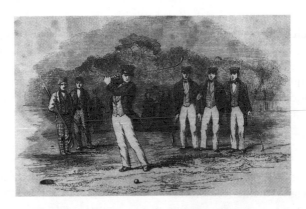

Golf as it was played in Scotland, *c.* 1858

Football has taken the place of religion in Scotland.
ROBIN JENKINS
A Would-Be Saint, 1978

Rangers had drawn their warriors from all corners of
Scotland, lads from mining villages, boys from Ayrshire
farms, and even an undergraduate from the University of
Glasgow. Celtic likewise had ranged the industrial belt and
even crossed to Ulster and the Free State for men fit to win
matches so that dividends might accrue. But for such as
Danny they remained peerless and fearless warriors, saints
of the Blue or the Green as it might be; and in delight in
the cunning moves of them, in their tricks and asperities,
the men on the terraces found release from the drabness of
their own industrial degradation.
GEORGE BLAKE
The Shipbuilders, 1935

Playing at shiney is thus performed – an equal number of men drawn up on opposite sides, having clubs in their hands; each party has a Goal, and which party drives a wooden ball to their adversaries' Goal wins the game, which is rewarded by a share of a cask of Whiskey, on which both parties get drunk The players' legs being frequently broken, may give it the name of shiney.

SIR ENEAS MACINTOSH, EIGHTEENTH CENTURY
quoted in Roger Hutchinson, Camanachd, 1989

Golf is a thoroughly national game, it is as Scotch as haggis, cockie-leekie, high cheek-bones, or rowanberry jam.

ANDREW LANG
Lost Leaders, 1889

The grandest opportunity we had for skating in Scotland in my time was in the winter of 1880-81. That winter, ten miles of Loch Fyne at its head was frozen from shore to shore. We cruised on its jet-black polished surface as the Finns on any winter may cruise through the Aland isles in the Gulf of Bothnia ... Not till February, 1895, however, did I recover the first fine careless rapture of that marvellous winter on Loch Fyne ... Loch Lomond was frozen over and bearing by February 16. On that day I skated between Balloch and Inchmurrin. Special trains were run from Queen Street to Balloch and, 30,000 people were on the ice ... Booths, tents, and huxters' barrows lined the shore between the railway and Cameron House; a roaring business was being done in the hiring and fixing of skates and hot coffee, but there was not a single cigarette to be got ... Though cigarettes had come tentatively into use eight

years before, they were not yet a craze, and skaters would be
the last to look for them on the shores of Loch Lomond.

NEIL MUNRO
The Brave Days, 1931

Up! curlers, up! oor freen' John Frost
Has close his grip on loch an' lea:
Up! time's ower precious to be lost –
An' rally roon' the rink an' tee;
Wi' steady han', an' nerve, an' e'e –
Noo cannie, noo wi' micht and main,
To test by wick, an' guard an' draw
Oor prowess wi' the Channel-Stane.
O the roarin' Channel-Stane!
The cannie, creepin' Channel-Stane!
What music to the curler's ear
Like music o' the Channel-Stane.

JOHN USHER
'The Challen-Stane', *c.* 1850

Of a' the games that e'er I saw,
Man, callant, laddie, birkie, wean,
The dearest, far aboon them a'
Was aye the witching channel-stane.
Oh! for the channel-stane!
The fell good name the channel-stane!
There's no a game that e'er I saw
Can match auld Scotland's channel-stane.

JAMES HOGG
'The Channel-Stane', *c.* 1833

Off to a game of ice hockey *c.* 1880

O'er every hill, o'er every dale,
All by the winding banks of Tay,
Resounds the hunter's cheerful peel;
Their armour glittered to the day.
> JAMES MACPHERSON
> 'Earl Marischall's Welcome', *The Highlander*, 1758

I believe in God that all has wrocht
And create every thing of nocht;
And in his son, our Lord Jesu,
Who under Pilate tholit passioun
And deit for our salvatioun;
And on the third day rais again
As holy Scripture shöwis plain …
> SIR DAVID LYNDSAY OF THE MOUNT
> 'John the Commonweil's Creed', *Ane Pleasant Satyre
> of the Thrie Estaitis*, 1552

All love is lost but upon God alone.
> WILLIAM DUNBAR
> 'The Merle and the Nightingale', *c*. 1508

A man with God is always in the majority.
> JOHN KNOX
> inscription (translated from the French) on the
> Reformation Monument, Geneva, Switzerland.

It is in vain that I study the subject of the Scotch Church. I
have heard it ten times over from Murray, and twenty times
from Jeffrey, and I have not the smallest conception of
what it is about. I know it has something to do with
oatmeal, but beyond that I am in utter darkness.
> SYDNEY SMITH
> Lady Holland, *Memoir of Sydney Smith*, 1855

Damn
Aa.
> ALEXANDER SCOTT
> 'Scotch Religion.
> *Scotched*

But all Scotchmen are not religious ... some are theologians.
> GERALD BENDALL
> *Mrs James's Bonnet*, 1907

[The Scots] have a superstitious reliance on the efficacy of going constantly to church. Many of them may be said to pass their lives there; for they go almost without ceasing, and look so sorrowful ... as if they were going, not only to bury their sins, but themselves.
> CAPTAIN EDWARD TOPHAM
> *Letters from Edinburgh Written in the Years 1774 and 1775*

If they [the Kirk and its ministers] gave manhood and liberty to Scotland, they did much to sap the first and shackle the second. Condemning natural pleasures and affections, they drew a dark pall over the old merry Scottish world, the world of the ballads and the songs, of frolics and mummings and 'blithesome bridals', and, since human nature will not be denied, drove men and women to sinister and perverted outlets.
> JOHN BUCHAN, LORD TWEEDSMUIR
> *Witchwood*, 1927

You're either a dirty Orangeman or a Papist bastard. It's much more subtle than anti-Semitism, and it must be understood that most people in Glasgow don't spend much time thinking about it at all from one year's end to the next. But it's there, and even the most impartial Glaswegian is likely to have some feelings based on religion in this restricted sense.

CLIFF HANLEY
Dancing in the Streets, 1958

Spread women, ugly mean and little children
dressed in the Sunday best of bigotry,
suffered to come unto intolerance
down orange miles of bannered frippery;
the gadfly flutes, the goading fifes,
the yattering side-drums of expended wars
forcing sectarian division through
our public streets choked back with fuming cars.

MAURICE LINDSAY
'Glasgow Orange Walk'

A Sunday in Scotland is for the traveller like a thunderstorm at a picnic.

THEDOR FONTANE
Beyond the Tweed, Pictures and Letters from Scotland,
1860

We can't for a certainty tell
What mirth may molest us on Monday;
But, at least, to begin the week well,
Let us all be unhappy on Sunday.

CHARLES, LORD NEAVES
'Let us all be unhappy on Sunday', *Songs and Verses*,
1872

Entering your house, I sniff again
The Free Church air, the pictures on the wall
of ministers in collars, all these dull
acres of brown paint, the chairs half seen
in dim sad corners by the sacred hall

under the spread antlers of that head
mildly gazing above leathern tomes.
So many draperies in so many rooms.
So many coverlets on each heavy bed.
A stagnant green perpetuating these glooms.
IAIN CRICHTON SMITH
'Entering Your House'

Th' approach of Sunday still I can't but dread,
For still old Edinburgh comes into my head
Where on that day a dreary gloom appears
And the kirk bells ring doleful in your ears.
JAMES BOSWELL

To promote a woman to bear rule, superiority, dominion, or empire above any realm, nation, or city is repugnant to nature, contumely to God, a thing most contrarious to His revealed will and approved ordinance, and finally it is the subversion of good order, of all equity and justice.
JOHN KNOX
First Blast of the Trumpet Against the Monstrous Regiment of Women, 1558

It wasn't a woman who betrayed Jesus with a kiss.
CATHERINE CARSWELL
The Savage Pilgrimage, 1932

O Knox he was a bad man
he split the Scottish mind,
the one half he made cruel
and the other half unkind.
> ALAN JACKSON
> 'Knox'

When I entered the world there was one Knox deaving us a'
with his clavers, and now that I am going out of it, there is
one Clavers [Claverhouse] deaving us with his knocks.
> LADY ELPHINSTONE AT 103
> quoted by Sir Walter Scott in his journal, November
> 1827

There is not to be found, in all history, any miracle attested
by a sufficient number of men, of such unquestioned good
sense, education and learning, as to secure us against all
delusion in themselves; of such undoubted integrity, as to
place them beyond all suspicion of any design to deceive
others; of such credit and reputation in the eyes of
mankind, as to have a great deal to lose in case of their
being detected in any falsehood; and at the same time
attesting facts, performed in such a public manner, and in
so celebrated a part of the world, as to render the detection
unavoidable.
> DAVID HUME
> *The Philosophical Works of David Hume*, 1874-5

The ruins of St Blane's Chapel on the Isle of Bute

Nothing seems more certain than the loneliness of one's own self, which no mass hysteria, or political creed, or religious faith, can save from the last lonely departure that is death. It seems more than a pity to go out into that final dark without making some sort of effort to discover what glimmerings of harmony may visit the mind if we give it a reasonably receptive chance.

    NEIL M. GUNN
    Off in a Boat, 1938

One's religion is whatever he is most interested in, and yours is Success.

    J.M. BARRIE
    The Twelve-pound Look, 1910

If we lie down in the grave, the whole man a piece of broke machinery, to moulder with the clods of the earth – so be it, at least there is an end of pain, care, woes and wants; if that part of us called Mind, does survive the apparent destruction of the man – away with old-wife prejudices and tales! Every age and every nation has had a different set of stories ...

ROBERT BURNS
letter to Robert Muir, 7 March 1788

Enjoy the present; nor with needless cares
Of what may spring from blind misfortune's womb,
Appal the surest hour that life bestows.
Serene, and master of yourself, prepare
For what may come; and leave the rest to Heaven.

DR JOHN ARMSTRONG
The Act of Preserving Health, 1744

Immortality! Why, the most of us don't know what to do with this one little personal life, and might well wonder how we came to be promoted to the dignity thereof, the claim to immortality is the claim to be trusted with millions of pounds because one has shown himself unfit to be trusted with sixpence.

JAMES THOMSON ('B.V.')
Essays and Phantasies, 1887
'Ane by Ane'

No man lives without jostling and being jostled; in all ways he has to elbow himself through the world giving and receiving offence.

THOMAS CARLYLE
On Boswell's Life of Johnson, 1832

Where are our fathers? Whither gone
The mighty men of old?
The patriarchs, prophets, princes, Kings,
In sacred books enrolled?

Gone to the resting-place of man,
The everlasting home,
Where ages past have gone before,
Where future ages come.

MICHAEL BRUCE
'The Complaint of Nature', *Poems on Several Occasions*, 1770

Farewell, kind-hearted dogmatising friend,
who undervalued 'life on earth below'
in hope of 'lasting glories' at the end.
If right, you're there at heaven's non-stop show,
waiting to greet me – *See! It's all I claimed* …
Pity you never got your doubting tamed –
as ticketless, I'm ushered down below.
If wrong – why, neither of us will ever know!

MAURICE LINDSAY
'A Minister of Religion'

Here lie I, Martin Elginbrod
Have mercy on my soul, Lord God;
As I would do were I Lord God
And you were Martin Elginbrod.

GEORGE MACDONALD
David Elginbrod, 1863

I'll ha'e nae hauf-way hoose, but aye be whaur
Extremes meet – it's the only way I ken
To dodge the curst conceit o' bein' richt
That damns the vast majority o' men.
HUGH MACDIARMID
A Drunk Man Looks at the Thistle, 1926

Thoch raging stormes move us to shake,
And wind mak waters us o'er flow;
We yield thereto, but do not break,
And in the calm unbent we grow!

So, baneist men, (thoch princes rage),
And prisoners, be not despairit.
Abide the blast whill that it 'suage;
For time sic causis has repairit.
ANON
'The Reeds in the Loch Sayīs', *The Maitland Manuscript*, 1582

I do not think the road to contentment lies in despising
what we have not got. Let us acknowledge all good, all
delight that the world holds, and be content without it.
GEORGE MACDONALD
Annals of a Quiet Neighbourhood, 1867

And, as I roon the corner, best of a'
The mavis, singing on my gavel wa' –
Happy am I, altho' I bide my lane,
To ha'e a singin' hert that's a' my ain.
HELEN CRUICKSHANK
'Corstorphine Woods'

In anguish we uplift
A new unhallowed song;
The race is to the swift,
The battle to the strong.
>   JOHN DAVIDSON
>   'War Song'

Children are taught, this leader or that king
built castles and scored victories, his battle scars
honour and guilt, inextricably mixed.
Who laid the stones, put death into his wars?
>   MAURICE LINDSAY
>   'Responsibilities'

Have all our revolutions, all our changes of creed, all the
bloodshed and the burning, made men happier?
>   ANDREW LANG
>   *St Andrews*, 1893

Man's inhumanity to man
Makes countless thousands mourn.
>   ROBERT BURNS
>   'Man Was Made to Mourn', 1786

O! we're a' John Tamson's bairns,
We're a' John Tamson's bairns;
There ne'er will be peace till the warld again
Has learn'd to sing wi' micht and main,
We're a' John Tamson's bairns.
>   DR JOSEPH ROY
>   'John Tamson was a merry old Earl', *c.* 1870

Here's freedom to him that wad read;
Here's freedom to him that wad write!
There's nane ever feared that the truth should be heard
But they wham the truth wad indite.
ROBERT BURNS
'Here's a health to them that's awn'

The world is neither Scottish, English, nor Irish, neither
French, Dutch, nor Chinese, but *human*, and each nation
is only the partial development of a universal humanity.
JAMES GRANT
on founding the *National Association for the
Vindication of Scottish Rights*, 1852

All the world's a-gadding,
Running madding;
None doth his station hold.
He that is below envieth him that riseth,
He that is above, him that's below dispiseth;
So every man his plot and counter-plot deviseth,
Hallo, my fancy, whither wilt thou go?
WILLIAM CLELAND
'Hello, my fancy'

Maist pleasour purchest is by price of pain.
Those that indures the winter's sharp assay
Sall see the seemly simmer shine again.
JOHN STEWART OF BALDYNNEIS
'Live still heirfore', *Rhapsodies of the Author's Youthful
Braine*, 1586

The world is so full of a number of things,
I'm sure we should all be as happy as kings.
> ROBERT LOUIS STEVENSON
> 'Happy Thoughts', *A Child's Garden of Verses*, 1885

Let neist day come as it thinks fit,
The present minute's only ours.
> ALLAN RAMSAY
> 'Look up to Pentland's Tow'ring Tap'

Truth should not be spoken at all times.
> SIR WALTER SCOTT
> journal, 1827

If you praise a man you please only himself. In order to provide the greatest happiness for the greatest number, you must damn with faint praise, for then you please all a man's friends.
> JOHN DAVIDSON
> *Sentences and Paragraphs*, 1893

I knew a very wise man so much of Sir Chr–'s sentiment, that he believed if a man were permitted to make all the ballads, he need not care who should make the laws of a nation.
> ANDREW FLETCHER OF SALTOUN
> letter to the Marquis of Montrose and Others, 1703

Poverty! Thou half-sister of Death, thou cousin-german of Hell, where shall I find force of execration equal to thy demerits!
> ROBERT BURNS
> letter to Peter Hill, 17 January 1791

Carrick Castle, Lochgoilhead, a former royal stronghold hereditarily kept
by the Argyll family

To make a happy fireside clime
To weans and wife,
That's the true pathos and sublime
Of human life.
>   ROBERT BURNS
>   'Epistle to Dr Blacklock'

Gie aa, and aa comes back
wi mair nor aa
Hain ocht, and ye'll hae nocht,
aa flees awa.
>   DOUGLAS YOUNG
>   'Luve'

The bells on New Year's morning
Strike twelve and then are dumb;
Now lover turns to lover
With thoughts of days to come.

Now old folks sigh and wonder,
'Who sees the next year dawn?'
And wise folk say, 'There's comfort
Though half the best be gone.'

While one guest all unbidden
Keeps whispering in my ear,
'When little's left to hope for,
The less will be to fear.'

    MARION ANGUS
    'New Year's Morning'

Werena my heart licht I wad dee.
    LADY GRIZEL BAILLIE
    refrain of song, 1724

Mrs St Clair ... gave birth to a daughter, which as Mr St
Clair sensibly remarked, though not so good as a boy, was
yet better than nothing at all.
    SUSAN FERRIER
    The Inheritance, 1824

If ye want a boy, dae it wi yer buits on.
    DUNDEE SAYING

Remember that the theatre of the world is wider than the realm of England.

> MARY, QUEEN OF SCOTS
> before her judges, October 1586

Here Aretino lies, most bitter gall,
Who whilst he lived spoke ill of all;
Only of God the arrant Scot
Naught said, but that he knew him not.

> ATTRIBUTED TO WILLIAM DRUMMOND OF
> HAWTHORNDEN, *c.* 1681

Once in a saintly passion
I cried with desperate grief,
'O Lord, my heart is black with guile,
Of sinners I am chief.'
Then stooped my guardian angel
And whispered from behind,
'Vanity, my little man,
You're nothing of the kind.'

> JAMES THOMSON ('B.V.')
> *A Voice from the Nile*, 1884

This field of stones, he said,
May well call forth a sigh;
Beneath them lie the dead,
On them the living lie.

> JAMES THOMSON ('B.V.')
> 'In a Christian Churchyard', *National Reformer*, 1877

It's ill taking the breeks off a Highland man.

> SIR WALTER SCOTT
> *Rob Roy*, 1817

Gourock, the Clyde sea-bathing resort and, later,
steamer (now ferry) terminal

Eve and the apple was the first great step in experimental
science.
JAMES BRIDIE
Mr Bolfrey, 1843

The first wife calls the next 'a whining trollop':
I like both wives. It's him I'd like to wallop!
G.S. FRASER
'Two Wives, One Husband'

82

Pride never yet left
His feir but a fall.
> SIR RICHARD HOLLAND
> *The Howlett, c.* 1475

If folk think I'm mean, they'll no' expect too much.
> SIR HARRY LAUDER

The man that will nocht when he may
Shall have nocht when he wald.
> ROBERT HENRYSON
> 'Robene and Makyne', *c.* 1460

Surfeits slay mair than swords.
> OLD SCOTS SAYING

All things helps (quod the Wren) when she pished in the
sea.
> DAVID FERGUSSON
> *Scottish Proverbs*, 1641

Thae half said. Quhat say thai? Let them say.
> GEORGE KEITH, 5th EARL MARISCHAL
> family motto, Marischal College, Aberdeen, founded
> 1593
> (also, Englished, over George Bernard Shaw's
> fireplace)

Be sure ye dinna quit the grip
Of ilka joy when ye are young,
Before auld age your vitals nip,
And lay ye twafauld o'er a rung.
> ALLAN RAMSAY
> after Horace

It requires a surgical operation to get a joke well into a Scotch understanding. Their only idea of wit, or rather that inferior idea of that electric talent which prevails occasionally in the North, and which under the name of *wut*, is so infinitely distressing to people of good taste, is laughing immoderately at stated intervals. They are so imbued with metaphysics that they even make love metaphysically; I overheard a young lady of my acquaintance, at a dance in Edinburgh, exclaim, in a sudden pause of the music, 'What you say, my Lord, is very true of love in the abstract,' – here the fiddles began fiddling furiously, and the rest was lost.

SYDNEY SMITH
Lady Holland, Memoir of Sydney Smith, 1855

I scarcely ever heard a Scotchman tell a good story ... for, notwithstanding he might put in all the circumstances to whorl it to a point, he would be sure to spoil it by his deficiency in manner, and remove the sting, which ought to tickle the imagination of the hearer, by appearing not to feel it himself.

CAPTAIN EDWARD TOPHAM
Letters from Edinburgh Written in the Years 1774 and 1775

There are two things a Highlander likes naked, and one of them is malt whisky.

OLD SAYING
quoted by F. Marian McNeill in *The Scots Cellar*, 1956

There's meat and music here, as the fox said when he stole the bagpipes.

OLD SAYING

quoted by W. Gordon Smith in *This is My Country*, 1976

A minister in a rural parish ... when out walking a day or two after his return from the General Assembly in Edinburgh was accosted by one of his parishioners. 'I've just been up to the station, sir, and I see there's a wooden box lying there addressed to you.'

'Quite so, Tammas, quite so. Just a few books I was buying when I was in Edinburgh.'

'Aye. Imphm. Ah well, sir, I wadna be owre lang. They're leakin'.'

ANON

quoted in F. Marian McNeill, *The Scots Cellar*, 1956

I wish I were a brewer's horse:
Then when the coast was clear
I'd turn my head where tail should be
And drink up all the beer.

ANON

A parody of a Prencentor's rhyme, to the tune 'Crimond', from the nineteenth century, when it was still considered irreverent to sing the words of the Psalms during choir practice.

Humff hamff quod the Laird of Bamf

DAVID FERGUSSON

Scottish Proverbs, 1641

From Kenmore
To Ben Mohr
The land is a' the Markiss's;
The mossy howes,
The heathery knowes,
And ilka bonnie park is his.
The bearded goats,
The tozie stots,
An' a' the braxy carcases;
Ilk crofter's rent,
Ilk tinkler's tent,
An' ilka collie's bark is his;
The muir-cock's craw,
The piper's blaw,
The gillie's hard day's work is his;
From Kenmore
To Ben Mohr
The warld is a' the Markiss's!

> JAMES MACTAVISH OF WATERSIDE, DOUNE
> on the vast possessions of the Marquis of Breadalbane
> in 1901

The earth belongs unto the Lord
And all that it contains,
Excepting all the Western Isles
And they are all MacBrayne's.

> POPULAR RHYME
> probably dating from the early years of the twentieth
> century, against the monopoly shipping company
> David MacBrayne Limited, elsewhere wittily referred
> to by Magnus Magnusson as 'the strangle of the Isles'.

Fishing from a riverbank early in the nineteenth century

She just wore
Enough for modesty – no more.
ROBERT BUCHANAN
'White Rose and Red'

Roseberry to his lady says,
'My hinnie and my succour,
O shall we do the thing ye ken,
Or shall we take our supper?'

Wi' modest face, sae fu' o' grace,
Replied the bonny lady;
'My noble lord do as you please,
But supper is na ready.'
ANON, EIGHTEENTH CENTURY
quoted by Burns in *The Merry Muses of Caledonia*

See how the poet, fired by love divine,
Swives in the barley, full of barley wine,
Whilst in the lane, impassioned by Five Star,
Some lawyer's at it in his Jaguar.
    ROBERT GARIOCH
    'Love à la Mode'

The Minester said it wald dee,
the cypress buss I plantit.
But the buss grew til a tree,
naething dauntit.

It's growan, stark and heich,
derk and straucht and sinister,
kirkyairdielike and dreich.
But whaur's the Minister?
    DOUGLAS YOUNG
    'Last Lauch', *Auntran Blads*, 1943

On Waterloo's ensanguined plain
Full many a gallant man was slain.
But none, by sabre or by shot,
Fell half as flat as Walter Scott.
    ANON
    on Scott's *Field of Waterloo*, 1815

Here lies the bones of Elizabeth Charlotte,
Born a virgin, died a harlot.
She was aye a virgin at seventeen,
A remarkable thing in Aberdeen
    ORAL TRADITION

Nowhere beats the heart so kindly
as beneath the tartan plaid.
> WILLIAM EDMONDSTOUNE AYTOUN
> on Prince Charles Edward Stuart at Versailles, 1849

Och, what's the annual Mod now? Just a society function
the success of which is judged by the amount of money it
makes. And anyway, what is the use of keeping a language
alive for a dying people?
> COMPTON MACKENZIE
> *The North Wind of Love*, part of a conversation set in
> 1911

For nought can cheer the heart sae weel,
As can a canty Hieland reel;
It even vivifies the heel
To skip and dance:
Lifeless is he who canna feel
Its influence.
> ROBERT FERGUSSON
> 'The Daft Days'

Pipes are in the house to-night;
put kitchen table to the wall;
we'll dance a reel before we part
a dram behind and a dram before ...

The pipes are clappering in the house;
here's one joy among us still.
We'll dance before the island sinks;
and let the boat sail if she will.
> ADAM DRINAN
> *Women of the Happy Island*, 1944

A bagpipe concert early in the nineteenth century

A hermit, suffering all its wrongs alone,
The heart remains within its bower of bone.
RUTHVEN TODD
'The Darkling Plain', *Garland for the Winter Solstice*,
1961

Stories to rede are delitabill,
Suppose that thai be nocht but fabill.
JOHN BARBOUR
The Bruce, 1375

I have no great faith in the boastful pretensions to intuitive
propriety and unlaboured elegance. The rough material of
Fine Writing is certainly the gift of Genius; but I as firmly
believe that the workmanship is the united effort of Pain,
Attention, and repeated Trial.
ROBERT BURNS
letter, probably to Henry Erskine, 22 February 1789

Visual and auditory memories of childhood are always sorted and touched up in later years. We remember that we remember. Our memory pictures, like all acts of will, are shamelessly dishonest.

> JAMES BRIDIE
> *One Way of Living*, 1939

Within this circular idea
Call'd vulgarly a tomb,
The ideas and impressions lie
That constitute Hume.

> ANON
> on the Circular Monument on Edinburgh's Calton
> Hill to the philosopher David Hume

O grant me, Heaven, a middle state
Neither too humble nor too great;
More than enough for Nature's ends,
With something left to treat my friends.

> DAVID MALLET (1705?-1765)
> 'Imitation of Horace'

Here under this sod and under these trees
Is buried the body of Solomon Pease.
But here in this hole lies only his pod
His soul is shelled out and gone up to God.

> EPITAPH IN A FALKIRK CEMETERY

The party's almost over. Though at times a trifle odd
I've thoroughly enjoyed it. Thank you for having me,
God.

> MAURICE LINDSAY

To all, to each, a fair good-night,
And pleasing dreams, and slumbers light!
    SIR WALTER SCOTT
    Marmion, 1808

Here's to the year that's awa'!
We will drink it in strong and in sma'!;
And here's to ilk bonnie young lassie we lo'ed,
Where swift flew the year that's awa'.
    JOHN DUNLOP
    'The Year That's Awa', 1850

Gude nicht, and joy be wi' you a'.
    CAROLINE OLIPHANT, LADY NAIRNE
    'Gude Nicht'

The traveller has regrets
For the receding shore …

The blue lights on the hill,
The white lights in the bay
Told us the meal was laid
And that the bed was made
And that we could not stay.
    G.S. FRASER
    'The Traveller has Regrets', *Collected Poems*, 1961

For auld lang syne, my dear,
For auld lang syne,
We'll tak a cup o kindness yet
For auld lang syne.
    ROBERT BURNS
    'Auld Lang Syne', *Scots Musical Museum*, 1796

Holyrood House, Edinburgh's royal palace, *c.* 1826

Glossary

auntran, autrin – various
braxy – sheep disease
breid – bread
brissit brawnis – swollen limbs
causeys – street-edges
channel-stane – curling stone
clachan – village
clanjamfrie – crowd
a cogie o' yill – a measure of ale
considerand – considering
crans – a measure of fish
cushat – pigeon
delitabill – enjoyable
dreich – grim
feir – companion
Five Star – high octane petrol
flyting – abuse
gash – lively
gif – if
hirples – limps
hoasts – coughs
ilk – each
joe – sweetheart
kendillt – kindled
lauch – laugh
lear – learning

lintin – relaxed
loon – boy
lowest – brightest
maks – mingles
pat – pot
pennywheep – a small measure of ale
pickle bit – little bit
piece – jam sandwich
quod – said
routh – plenty
runklet – crinkled
skaichen – scavenging
snell – sharp
spulyie – plunder
sweel – whirl-around
synhalt – limping
tholit – endured
thrang – busy
tozie – tousled
vennels – narrow lanes
venust – love or begotten
waistie wanis – spoiled children
whilk – which
wyson – gizzard